To help you

free

YOU KNOW YOU'RE A **CHILD** OF THE **50**s WHEN...

Helen Lincoln

summersdale

YOU KNOW YOU'RE A CHILD OF THE 50s WHEN...

Summersdale Publishers Ltd
46 West Street
Chichester
West Sussex
PO19 1RP
UK

www.summersdale.com

Printed and bound in China

ISBN: 978-1-84953-160-3

Substantial discounts on bulk quantities of Summersdale books are available to corporations, professional associations and other organisations. For details contact Summersdale Publishers by telephone: +44 (0) 1243 771107, fax: +44 (0) 1243 786300 or email: nicky@summersdale.com.

To....................................

From................................

You know you're a child of the 50s when…

You can still do a perfect
Elvis lip curl, believing
that it thrills the ladies.

You are one of the few
people who can distinguish
the balls in snooker on a
black and white TV screen.

You can remember
your mum wiping your
face with a corner of
her apron – no need for
antibacterial soap in
those days!

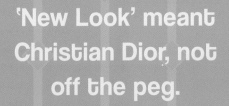

'New Look' meant Christian Dior, not off the peg.

You still eat all your dinner – due to constant threats as a child that you'd be eating it in your sandwiches the next day if you didn't.

You know all the words to
'Bless Your Beautiful Hide'
and fall about laughing
if you hear the line, 'No,
Frank, them's *Mormons.*'

You have flashbacks of the Festival of Britain every time you visit the South Bank Centre.

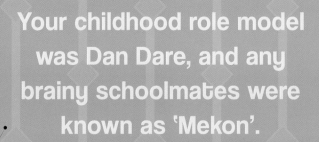

Your childhood role model
was Dan Dare, and any
brainy schoolmates were
known as 'Mekon'.

Your idea of classic
elegance is a cashmere
twinset in a pastel colour.

You can still remember
milk being delivered by
horse and cart.

You only saw computers
in films and they took up
an entire room.

You still hold doors open for women.

Your toys were mechanical,
not battery-powered.

You remember the time you really could get away from it all and there were no answer machines, emails or texts – if you were out, you were out.

It snowed just as much
on TV as it did outside.

You still love Lucy.

You remember the day sweet-rationing ended – luckily, you also grew up in an era of free NHS dentistry!

You would spend the day
with your hair in rollers if
you had a date
that night.

Elvis and Marilyn were
your role models, and have
never been bettered.

You found your thrill on
Blueberry Hill.

You can remember what you were doing the day James Dean died.

You spent Saturday nights 'necking' in the back row of the cinema.

Your parents thought
nothing of you going off
to play with your friends
for the day.

You were really excited
to earn £3 a week in your
first job.

Your dad drove a Fiat 500 'Nuova'.

You miss 'going to work
on an egg'.

You are still proud that you could keep a hula hoop up for the longest out of all your friends.

You remember worrying that you would be called up for National Service.

You thought you were at the height of technology listening to *The Light Programme* on a radio that was bigger than most of today's microwaves.

Your parents bought their first TV specifically to watch the Coronation.

Your school never offered you 'careers advice'.

You habitually stand next to the base unit of your phone for hours talking to someone, even though you've had a cordless for years.

You used to fantasise about a magic way to work out square roots without having to use a slide rule.

You remember eating packets of Rice Krispies without Snap, Crackle and Pop on the box.

You have never asked or been asked, 'What does your mum do for a living?'

You are still baffled as to why the rotary-dial telephones had '9' at the far end, so it would take 30 seconds to call the emergency services.

Your idea of a 'girls' night' was three of you doing needlework by the electric heater.

You made a Mr Turnip
with an electric light bulb,
as seen on *Whirligig*.

You cried the day they killed off Grace Archer.

The words 'Are you sitting comfortably? Then I'll begin...' still fill you with warmth and happiness.

Your idea of a 'laptop' involves a lot less technology and far fewer clothes.

Your mum used to pack you off to school with a soggy sandwich in the new container she got from her latest Tupperware party.

You believe that no April Fool's joke will ever outdo the *Panorama* spaghetti harvest.

You still refer to *Strictly Come Dancing* as '*Come Dancing*', and frequently wonder aloud what happened to Sylvia Peters.

You made the embarrassing mistake of asking for coffee and croissants for two at Tiffany's on your first trip to New York.

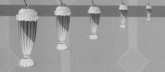

You would eat your dinner on a TV tray on Fridays just to hear, 'It's Friday, it's five o'clock... it's *Crackerjack*!'

You had to go to the emergency room after choking on the little plastic toy in your cornflakes.

You and your friends
would spend hours
watching a metal spring
slink down the stairs.

You tried everything you could possibly imagine to replicate chrome and fins on your first car.

You once owned a conical bra and dreamed of being Jane Russell…

... or, if you were a boy, you wanted your girlfriend to wear a conical bra just like Jane Russell.

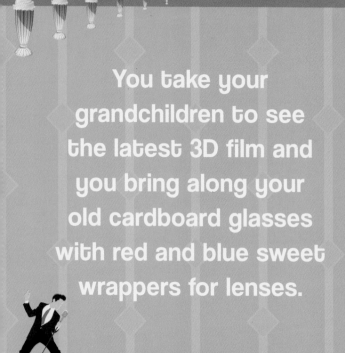

You take your grandchildren to see the latest 3D film and you bring along your old cardboard glasses with red and blue sweet wrappers for lenses.

You spent your school PE lessons trying to run as fast as Roger Bannister.

You still think the scariest film of all time is *The Day the Earth Stood Still.*

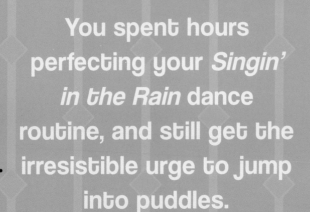

You spent hours perfecting your *Singin' in the Rain* dance routine, and still get the irresistible urge to jump into puddles.

Your parents told you to steer clear of Teddy boys, and you're still suspicious of people in winkle-pickers.

You once looked forward to receiving the next I-Spy Club books and badges in the post.

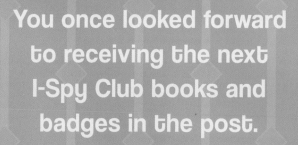

You were amazed
that the child on the
Rowntree's 'Don't forget
the fruit gums, Mum!'
advert was allowed to
demand sweets from
his mother.

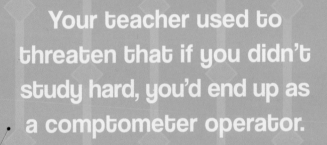

Your teacher used to threaten that if you didn't study hard, you'd end up as a comptometer operator.

You would race to school on a Friday morning to discuss the latest antics of the Bash Street Kids in *The Beano*.

You remember first seeing Lego in the shops and thinking, 'This will never catch on...'

You still feel obliged to follow the weekly dinner schedule from your childhood: Sunday – roast, Monday – cold meat, Friday – fish and chips. Deviations are unacceptable.

You and all your friends
owned miniature toy
farms, and you would save
up your pocket money to
buy a new plastic cow.

You remember having
weird dreams about dogs
in space.

You miss seeing public information films about road safety, table manners, and how to stop coughs and sneezes spreading diseases.

You remember playgrounds as a place for hopscotch, skipping and games of kiss-chase, not kids using their mobile phones or listening to iPods.

You flinch at the sight of a wooden ruler, a plimsoll, or anything else once used as a means of 'discipline' at school.

You know how to have fun without sitting at a computer.

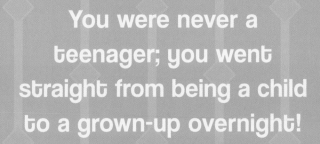

You were never a teenager; you went straight from being a child to a grown-up overnight!

You remember crowding into a 'listening room' at the local record shop to hear the latest sounds from Dickie Valentine and Frankie Laine.

You had 'conquer Everest'
on your to-do list.

You used to dream that people could go to the Moon – but you knew it would never really happen.

You have an extensive
collection of Turf
cigarette cards.

You wanted to be a
beatnik, not a clean-cut kid.

Nigel Molesworth was your hero and you're still convinced that your school was the model for St Custard's.

The most shocking thing for a girl to be was 'fast'.

You were proud of your horn-rimmed specs – they made you look so intellectual!

Unlike Frank Sinatra and Celeste Holm in *High Society*, you *did* want to be a millionaire.

Hearing Joyce Grenfell saying 'George, don't do that!' takes you straight back to your school days.

You still know how to
play a washboard, thanks
to your involvement in
the skiffle craze.

You know how to conjugate lots of Latin verbs – but you still don't know what the point of learning them was, as you've never met anyone who speaks Latin.

Dressing up for a date used to involve drainpipe trousers (for him) and a polka-dot skirt with a net petticoat (for her).

Your grandchildren's experience of school seems worlds away from your own. They've got central heating now, for a start!

You had flying ducks on the wall (and it wasn't an ironic statement).

If someone tells you the colour of their new car, you always expect the word 'and' to be used.

You still call the radio 'the wireless' and wish the news bulletins today were delivered in the Queen's English.

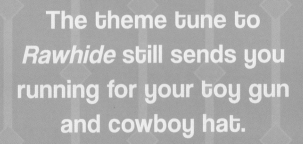

The theme tune to *Rawhide* still sends you running for your toy gun and cowboy hat.

You Know You're a Child of the 60s When...

Mark Leigh and Mike Lepine

ISBN: 978-1-84953-161-0

£4.99

Hardback

You Know You're a Child of the 70s When...

Mark Leigh and Mike Lepine

ISBN: 978-1-84953-162-7

£4.99

Hardback

You Know You're a Child of the 80s When...

Mark Leigh and Mike Lepine

ISBN: 978-1-84953-163-4

£4.99

Hardback

You Know You're a Child of the 90s When...

Helen Lincoln

ISBN: 978-1-84953-164-1

£4.99

Hardback

www.summersdale.com